# Southpaw

Also by Adrian Lane and published by Ginninderra Press
*Face to Face*

Adrian Lane

# Southpaw

## A Matter of Reversal

*Southpaw: A Matter of Reversal*
ISBN 978 1 74027 533 0
Copyright © Adrian Lane 2008
Cover photo by Alison Courtney: Gordon-Conwell, Winter
Author photo: Devan Foster

First published 2008
Reprinted with revisions 2009
Reprinted 2016

### Ginninderra Press
PO Box 3461 Port Adelaide 5015
www.ginninderrapress.com.au

# Contents

| | |
|---|---|
| Left-handers | 9 |
| Old Sports | 11 |
| Are You an Elephant? | 13 |
| Melbourne: Summer 2002 | 15 |
| Sheep People | 17 |
| Hume Landscape | 19 |
| Southern Christmas | 22 |
| Kangaroo | 23 |
| Hunter Summer | 24 |
| Preserving Pleasures | 26 |
| Memories of Beograd | 27 |
| Police Station | 29 |
| Welcome to Australia: Exodus 22:21 | 30 |
| Soldiers Bathing | 31 |
| A Saline Bath, RAF Hospital | 32 |
| Battle of Arakan, 1943… | 33 |
| The Glistening | 34 |
| Winter | 35 |
| Waiting | 36 |
| AA 164 | 38 |
| Toxic Care | 40 |
| Reading Room 368, Luce Library | 41 |
| Snow | 42 |
| The Dating Game | 43 |
| Sylvia | 44 |
| Loneliness | 45 |
| High Wire | 47 |
| Anna | 48 |
| The Fountain: Variations on a theme from Cowper | 49 |
| The Garden | 51 |

| | |
|---|---|
| The Chief Priests Chose For Power | 52 |
| Barrack Room: Matthew 27:24–31 | 53 |
| Stormstiller | 54 |
| The New Jonah | 55 |
| For Sandy and Sal | 56 |
| Skyspinners | 57 |
| Embracing Peniel | 58 |
| A Father's Love | 59 |
| Making the New Man | 64 |
| The Motherless Man | 66 |
| On the Ordination of a Friend | 67 |
| Towpath Symphony | 70 |
| Brokenback | 71 |

for my parents:

lovers of life,

givers of love

# Left-handers

We're a little different – left-handers.

It's not just that we wear our watches on the wrong arm
Or smudge our books
And so write cacky-handedly.
It's not just that scissors and irons make us feel clumsy
Or the belt's the wrong way
And the keys the wrong side.

We're always reminded we're round the wrong way,
So much that we take it for granted:
Each time we sit down the knife has to be switched
And the glasses are set – dare we move them?

We're forever a problem for coaches and teachers:
'First try it out right –
Oh well, I can't help you.'
You're just a bit odd, a bit weird, a bit gauche.
Clumsy and clunky, you know!
You can't buy the clubs
Or the sticks or the bats
And no one can teach you to throw!

Some even say sinister,
At the wrong hand.
You can't even shake on it, right!

And why are people more afraid of the left
And of being left out, not right on?
As though the right's right
And the rest are left over,
Raising the wrong hand,
Putting the wrong foot forward.

But we do think differently – it's true.
We like languages, music, spaces too.
We're creative
And maybe a mite more sensitive,
'Cause we know what it is to be different,
Yet forced into others' shoes;
So our worlds are a side more complex –
And that's our gift to you.

# Old Sports

It's so hard to say goodbye
to the sports of yesteryear.
I really can't face it,
admit – I'll no longer
run marathons round Mt Panorama
in those chunky trainers
or lie panting, puffing
on my back in singlet and running shorts
after giving my all
in 400-metre sprints, relays
in leathery spikes splitting at the seams
or sneak in drop shots
just above the tin
on those coin-operated courts at P.A.
It seems sacrilege to throw out these red sweatbands,
garbage the jockstrap you haven't used for years
or these stretched Speedos,
the wooden tennis racquet
famous for my left-handers;
even the carabiners from rock-climbing days
and my canoe bag
I need to keep as souvenirs:
old mementoes of energy,
of enjoying a body
that disappears so fast
and now so enviously watches others
who jump for the joy of it in their skins
and hang so lightly
to their wasted beauty.

If clothes maketh the man
this man is undone
as I tear from my drawers
these worn relics of athletic years
savoured, the more sweetly,
only in their passing.

for P.R.S.

## Are You an Elephant?

Are you an elephant,
Strong and wise?
Or are you an eagle,
With fantastic eyes?

Maybe you're a tiger
Striped orange and black?
Or maybe you're a chimpanzee
With a baby on its back?

Perhaps you're a koala
With a soft brown nose?
Or maybe you're a fruit bat
Hanging by your toes?

> *Are you in your jammies?*
> *Have you cleaned your teeth?*
> *'Cause it's nearly time to say goodnight*
> *And let these animals get some sleep.*

Now all these different animals
You'll find them at the zoo,
With bears and seals and crocodiles –
Which animal are you?

Perhaps you're a monkey,
Swinging through the trees?
Or maybe you're a camel
Carrying loads with clever knees?

Maybe you're the lion
With a great big roar?
Or maybe you're a slithering snake
Sliding 'cross the floor?

> *Are you in your jammies?*
> *Have you cleaned your teeth?*
> *'Cause it's nearly time to say goodnight*
> *And let these animals get some sleep.*

Perhaps you're a seagull,
High upon the mast?
Or maybe you're a panther,
Sleek and fast?

Maybe you're a tall giraffe,
Checking out the view?
Don't get behind that hippo!
He's about to do a — !   Phew!

Now all these different animals
Need to get some sleep;
Let's put them safe to bed now –
Shhh! Don't make a peep!

for Aidan

# Melbourne: Summer 2002

From the shortest day to the longest,
From snow to crunchy grass;
Dusty dry squares through a porthole;
Light. Bright light. Hurting the eyes.
And pale blue sky. High; so high.

Manic spending on Christmas presents;
Look both ways! Sorry!
It's back to walking on the left
And friendly service for no tips.

Federation Square. People everywhere!
A million critics: owning, eating
Crazed glass and snazzy floors,
Film and art, stone and tart.

Skin. Lots of it!
Healthy, toned and brown.
Singlets, shorts and sandals,
Calves and biceps too.
Rowers on the river,
Kissers in the parks,
Cricket…s and the cheep of birds,
Crispy, crunchy grass.

Oh my goodness! Half the MCG's gone!
Like a giant's slice of pavlova:
Flat and flaky white,
Sunken in the middle.
No more Daimaru,
No more Southern Cross,
But the QV cranes loom higher
And concrete's in the air.

New restaurants at the Docklands,
New building at the Shrine,
New gardens on the Yarra,
New chimes to chime a chime.
A new statue to John Landy,
New footballers to boot,
New roads, new trams across the tracks,
New Upper House, new Bracks!

Hot. Empty streets.
'Too hot for the flies!'
The tar melts.
The dog breath of the nor'-westerly teases the tennis banners.
'They've all gone to the beach!'
Or Fitzroy Pool.
But I've found the new Brunetti –
Still light at nine o'clock –
A little taste of Tuscany:
Come join me in the cool!

# Sheep People

Sheep people are just different –
they understand each other.
I mean, we love to sink our fingers
into a thick fleece
and feel that greasy wool;
we love our woolly jumpers, moleskins, oilskins
light on a dewy morning
checking the new ewes;
we love our lamb, the sales –
keeping an ear to the ground, an eye on the prices
always in for a yarn
under the Akubras.
We love our sheds, our yards, our dogs –
real dogs, working dogs, kelpies, collies
jumping sliding on the back of the ute
tongue puffing
before we've put our boots on –
you know, you can talk to a good dog –
it reads your mind.

We love the hum of the shed at shearing
penning the blighters up early lest they get wet
the shearers grinding, oiling combs and cutters
grabbing the legs, whoa! over you go
smoothing, shaving off that coat in easy strokes
pushing the naked thin scrawny beasts
raw-bottomed down the shutes
wide-eyed, bleating for their friends.
There's nothing better than throwing a fleece on the table
classing, into the bins
pressing a bale of AAA Merino
and stencilling its side,
loading the truck after a long year's wait –
'That'll pay another year of school fees –
just hope it rains.'

With thanks to David Campbell, *Work and Days*

# Hume Landscape

Christmas Eve:
A private ritual, long looked forward to;
A treat for the savouring:
We're on our way!

With the grunts of the trucks behind us
the road ahead
   opens up
   inviting
into a landscape replete with pleasures
   delicious with delights luscious and full
   banqueting the senses
      ever changing
      ever pleasing.

Cockatoos in a Nolan landscape feed and fight;
Hawks – or are they falcons? –
   wing with the wind:
   soaring, cruising, diving.
A wallaby, alert, stands to attention:
   its moist brown nose sniffing the breeze.

A train
   toyed with colourful containers chortles beside –
   its neat square edge Smartly cutting the country;
A gourmet sign promises pleasures;
A rest area amidst the trees:
   Ironbark; The Great Divide;
A view to Buffalo;
Leafy vines and mellow wines,
Lakes and art and golden mines.

Zooming through a mountain –
A car on an overpass speeds above
as in a film set quaintly made.

*A vision splendid:*
At the crest of each new cutting
laid out
panoramic vistas:
stunning
breathtaking
of rolling hills to the distance
   clumped by occasional trees
   sheltering Streeton sheep;
of Conder clouds in powder-blue skies;
of Gruner light playing with shadows
   as the sun sets on folded hills.

Speeded by. Rolling by.
Oh, if you could only stop each time
and breathe it in
and soak it in –
you could stay all day and not see all –
it's so vast,
   so rich,
   so grand –
beyond the capturing.

But the paired highway speeds on, flows on,
beautifully and carefully ribbon-groomed.

The night has come –
stealthed –
Beckett bright spots in the black
spill into sparkles of the glitzy city,
stop lights and loony hoons:
Sydney, here we come!

# Southern Christmas

The season's wrong, the reasons wrong
We only want to party
The light is long, the heat is high
Drought makes brown, wind makes dry:
No candles for a baby.

But the season's right, the reasons right
We must indeed have party
For God has come to heal his home
So sail and swim and rest and feast:
It's God who makes the party.

The flame's been lit, the darkness gasps
Soon will the serpent's head be crushed
This peasant king, this shepherd lamb
The others know and kneel before
Has made his home the undersphere
All for love's sake has chosen poor:
He's in our hands! –
Never will south be honoured more.

With thanks to Frank Houghton, *Thou who wast rich beyond all splendour*

for Verena

## Kangaroo

One-ten k on a no-moon night
with high beam off for an approaching car
His tall grey form emerges fast:
I hit the anchors hard.
He – blinded – curiously stares
then lopes away unscarred.

# Hunter Summer

It's been a ginger beer summer –
'with less sugar than your local orange juice'
It's not all bad – I mean –
It's 47 outside
and I'm fading fast!

It's been a shirts-off, barefoot summer,
a sticky sweaty summer,
a baking cooking summer,
an oven to the last.

It's been a thirsty summer
with snakes stuck in the tank,
a dry and itchy summer
so the water's fouled and rank.

It's been a bushfire summer
of gums with turned-up toes,
of cars corralled on freeways
and burnt out grapes in rows.

It's been a nasty northerly summer,
a gritty hot wind summer,
that's boiling up a storm
but can't make good its promises:
it spits and then is gone.

It's been a shrill cicada summer,
humming with the heat,
zzzimmering up and down the scales,
throbbing in their beat.

It's been a languid summer,
of social mooching cows
that sniff their lunch, then crunch, then munch,
then laze about for hours.

It's been a great goanna summer –
thick tail-tracks mark the dirt
tongue flicking licking ants are gone –
its sleepy eyes alert.

It's been a summer full of animals
bouncing 'cross the view:
come dusk we're always treated
to the penny kangaroo.

It's been an inside summer,
of bored and restless kids,
of inane talk, of sleepless nights,
thank God we've got the fridge!

## Preserving Pleasures

Adelaide, Summer 2007

Sagging branches press heavily 'gainst the shower window
Laden with Craig's bounty:
Delicious nectarines
Dangerously rescued from birds
On rickety stools and wonky ladders
Lest wasted
They thud drop
Squishy underfoot.

Scrumptiously stewed
Or delicately placed in clear bottles
Making pretty coloured patterns
Carefully boiled late into the night
To cool precious
Untouched for days
Stowed in dark caverns
Treasured
For wintry pleasures
With sweet friends.

for the Bromans

# Memories of Beograd

Of bulky ramparts, lit up, commanding
a Danube in flood;
of communist concrete dirty and drab;
of boulevards spacious and rubbished streets;
of luxuriant marble and metalled glass
amidst filthy beauties from an Icarus past.

Of teeming bus stations and trolleys grunting
humphing hot from distant eras
packed with old Australians eking out their pension cheques
   dinar by dinar;
of lawnmower Yugos scooting round sleek Mercedes;
of an empty airport
graveyarding remnants of heroic fighters
glorying in American bits and pieces
trophies from a war of lost pride.

Of scungy hotels with threadbare carpets
reeking of smoke;
of veal with a view
and paprika peppers with cream cheese –
drinking M beers, cherry yoghurts and raspberry frappes
so fresh you can taste this morning's market.

Of toothless toilet-minders in stinking holes
of wrinkled medieval peasants black-scarfed carting their
   vegetables
of Albanian beggars clutching babies to the breast;
of long-legged Nike lads cool in their sweats,
their swarthy uncles oozing a well-groomed masculinity:
burnished stubble and impeccable hair.

Of an unreadable Cyrillic script
distancing one empire, drawing another –
named for her evangelist
whose hope is history
archived with Roman relics
museumed for the tourist trade.

Of a National Theatre young and alive
producing classics, searching to make sense,
reinventing, wondering
who and where we are;
of borders in fertile fields
so new even the guards use builders' huts;
of war graves in no-man's land
so no man owns;
or is it so both own, and watch,
and neither will dare dig up pretending
others have never tilled this soil
which longs for a settled future
and tries to forget its past.

# Police Station

Osijek and Vukovar, Croatia

Who knows what silent horrors these grey walls have heard,
what secret tortures these bloodied walls have seen,
what bestial power unleashed,
fused by generations of unchained hate,
what seeds punch-planted in ugly fearful rule
by lonely kingdoms
behind rusting barbed wire
fencing out, fencing in, rounding up
neighbours
for traceless bakers' ovens.

Who knows what hidden wounds are borne,
what guilt carried?
For what?
No hate is satisfied, no myth undone,
no guilt purged or sin atoned.
Hate makes more hate
and guilt more guilt
in its violent unappeasing;
so all are victims still, all blame another
till someone shouts, 'Stop!'
and decides to love
brothers
made in His image.

# Welcome to Australia: Exodus 22:21

Port Augusta, South Australia

What silent hand has worked so we afraid
lock up in desert islands
to hide our shame from care?

Who conned the public's servants
to push from mind our care
those longing for a better life
who now in camps die scared?

Why soak another chapter
of shame into the land?
If law be broke attend
in lawful ways
But keep the wire for those who harm –
This razor double kills all kept behind
But harder cuts our hearts
For foreigners we too have been
And now make foreign Him who rules.

With thanks to Rosemary Laing, *Welcome to Australia*

# Soldiers Bathing*

by Will Ogilvie (Canadian War Museum 19710261-4759)

Look at these great gods: beautiful
who now can rest and laze
and wash away the stale sweat of war;

and comfort each other
in tenderness and love
though nothing be said –
cannot be said –
it is known
that we are brothers together
and fear and horrors,
for a breath,
are past.

With thanks to Anne Elder, *Regattas*

* The following three poems were written in response to artworks in the exhibition Shared Experience: Art and War – Australia, Britain and Canada in the Second World War, held at the Australian War Memorial, Canberra, Summer 2006.

# A Saline Bath, RAF Hospital

by A.R. Thomson (Imperial War Museum ART LD 3629)

He grips the bath
as each new wound
is seared by salt.
His tortured eye scars
this great god of a pilot
shot down naked
before a starched nurse
who dare not comfort
lest this hero
become a man.

# Battle of Arakan, 1943: Men of the 7th Rajput Regiment resting on South Hill with a parasol captured near Mayu River on the Rathedaung Front

by Anthony Gross (Imperial War Museum ART LD 3334)

While Japanese are standing
lying consumed
their geishas' parasols are swiped by stealthy Indians
who slink back into the night
tumescent
and now recover
to smugly stand
over flaccid foes.

# The Glistening

Late Tuesday
the street is silent –
its owners have retreated,
snugly snoring behind Victorian doors.
Three mates contented
from Paris-Go
welcome the warm rain
softly spotting
dropping dripping
smelling clean,
smudging slippery leaves
slicking steel covers with purple rainbows
painting Beckett nightscapes
of radiant lights
stills
freshly gleaming in the glistening.

for Jerome and Kim

# Winter

My knuckles tell me winter has arrived:
Fumbling with papers, unable to sort.
Skeleton trees expose clean edged vistas
Losing last leaves crunching, scuttling,
Crisp in Antarctic winds
Biting under cloudless skies
Chilling: keeping everybody in – fridges.
The heater struggles.
Condensation drops inside the windows
And won't wipe, but streaks
Like the morning mirror as I shiver shave.

Beanies have appeared.
Summer shorts and thin shirts
Exchanged for jackets, gloves and scarves.
A runny nose betrays Canute efforts with vitamins and shots
To ward off dark day worries.
Sure, some may be rum,
Snug with soup 'round open hearths –
Hibernating indoor types –
But I long for the warmth and the light
And keep my face grim when I hear,
'There'll be snow on the hills tonight!'

# Waiting

Good little boy
Bored
Waiting
At the Kombi after church
For siblings scattered
And for Mum and Dad to stop talking.

Tired little boy
On his own
Waiting
For the last bus
After late sports
On a freezing cold and scary night.

Teenagers
Hanging around
Waiting
For the right girls to turn up
Or having appeared
To change their mind, their man.

Always waiting
Waiting for what?
Till this job's done? This war's won?
Till there's money?
For the world to change? To come to him?
For something, I don't know what?

For joy? For death?
Till this world's done?
Why are we waiting?
Why not take the plunge?
Why not find the joy, the work and the prayer?
For what's won in the waiting is never lost
But what's lost in the waiting is never won.

## AA 164

The plane is full
Chock-a-block
Bulging, brimming with human flesh
Spilling from seats
Knocking, bumping, ''Scuse me, sir'
Babies, kids – twins! – on laps
And bags and bags and bags
Pushed in, stuffed in, shoved in overhead lockers
Underneath seats blocking access
'No standbys, no upgrades, no seat changes!'

Looking behind
I saw him
Still
Unmoving
Massive
A whale strapped to a cluttered beach
Expanding in all directions
Pressing the seat ahead.

I have to confess to selfish thinking,
'Thank God I'm not near him!'
But no one is.
A vacant seat.
A vacant seat?
He must have paid for two.
Can you do that?
How do you do that?
Two IDs? Two boarding cards?

And then the shame.
The spare seat screams,
'My pain! My pain!'

## Toxic Care

First Congregational Church, Greenwich, Connecticut

I heard today how good-hearted folks
packed barrels of clothes for cold Hawaiians.

But these grace-gifts galled,
Poisoned in their very seams with smallpox and pneumonia.

Lord, in my blind need keep me from such cruel care;
Make me find succour in your gentle love
And give me your eyes, clothed in humility.

# Reading Room 368, Luce Library

Princeton Seminary, New Jersey

There's a marvellous picture in each window today.
Framed by bold steel, the glass is so clear it is not there
And so, like unglazed oils, five paintings colour and texture
   the plain walls.

In one, the cross-topped steeple, slate and stone, points
   heavenward
Through thick shrubby greens into sapphire blue sky.
In another, rusty-red orange leaves almost paint over fresh
   yellows below,
Flecking and glistening in the sun and the breeze.
Behind, neat Georgian bricks with white windows stand for
   order and tradition –
Most Presbyterian.
To the left, two windows of dusty greens and browns play
   with each other
And the trees' grey trunks and branches are slowly formed
As in a puzzle nearly solved.
But to the right, Fall's work is done;
Few leaves left here: just the dead, waiting for the stronger
   wind
To leave contorted skeletons matt-greened with moss.

From Reading Room to Gallery.
More masterful than the Met.
Free for the seeing;
Yet only one time seen.
God's Gallery:
*Ad gloriam dei.*

# Snow

At last the snow has come.

Snowstorm warnings have sent men into mouseholes.
Sleet has turned to soft cotton wool flakes
that sting melt on the tongue
and are shaken off caps and coats like oversized confetti.

The world is silent.
Peaceful.
And quiet.

Cars too frightened to move turn slowly white
and merge into sidewalks lumpy-carpeted. No favourites here!
Trees make twiggy ice sculptures
and carry on their topsides fluffy white icing.
A crunching plough comes and goes
in a vain attempt to restore black road.

And still the world is quiet.

Snow motes floating under the light make specky shadows
and soft nothings as they land.
Yet nothings grow till squeaking underfoot
and rumbling off roofs – beware below!

Lights flicker.
And in the stillness the world is alert
and knows
that man is but nothing 'gainst a mighty God
who by soft nothings a whole new world makes
without having whispered one word.

# The Dating Game

I never was too good at competitive sports –
The competition bit.
Oh, I liked the play, the team, the sweat
But I just wasn't too fussed about winning;
I guess I felt for the loser –
So why be so cruel?
Give them the game.

No wonder I can't play the dating game –
Always pipped at the post, losing by a head.
In fact, I'm not even sure I know the rules:
I never seem to be playing quite right –
Always a bit out of position.
And I'm not even sure about the uniform.
It's not that I want to win –
It's just that I need a team;
And it's no fun always being picked last.

And who said it's a game?
It's no game!
This thing's for life!
And a minor mistake means major injuries.

Lord, help this lone lover find a forever friend,
Who'll play for joy and dare to share.

# Sylvia

Oh Sylvia,
How I love your love for life –
Light zest of joy-filled being.

Sing, Sylvia, sing!
Sing and fly to worlds unknown:
Exotic, rich and free.

How I have longed to nest with you.

But in your wonderful wildness
You did not wing with the wind,
But drifted,
Smashing hard into a cruel wall.

Two kids and a million dollars later
You manage, and control,
And step painfully around your scars and bruises.

And now I croon a lament
for your unhappy years,
your wounded spirit,
for Jamie and Susie pained by parents half a world apart,
and for my own pain,
at what could have been.

# Loneliness

I am surrounded by people, more people, worker bees
who play and laugh and love.
I watch
and hurt
and hold back hidden tears
and act a part.
Their love unknown lights my aloneness.

It is too shaming to share.
With whom?
Who wants a loser for a friend?

Outside my door attractive voices never seek out me.
Outside my door the sound of steps that come and go and
 come and go.

I wait.
Will they stop?
No one knocks.
I knock
and each knock back so gently heard cuts deep the wound
so one despises having knocked at all.

I long to touch, for touch, for love,
For commonplace and care
But my soul finds no friend
And self hangs out with self –
A lone goldfish in an other world.

Despair sinks further.
My vision skews.
Save this lone loser from his inner world
living a half-life beneath thickening scars.

The crocuses and robins are my friends.

## High Wire

I walk the high wire high,
Splendid to those afar;
But to those in the know
Balancing
Very precariously,
Very ominously,
Grieving the route having gone,
Cursing the no turning back.

# Anna

For Tim and Poppy

I don't believe it –
How can it be
That such a friend
Can join us no longer
For cards and cheese
And a cheeky retort?

How can it be
That one with such a heart for God
Will never again
Delight in my sermons
And spark an insight
Fresh and pithy?

How can it be
That one with such a winsome word of life for all
Should suddenly be stopped;
A sun gone out
A smile now hidden?

But this I know – for sure –
That she has crossed from death to life
Not once, but twice;
And while we wait, and long to join her
There's work and joy to find and do
This other side of heaven.


John 5:24

# The Fountain: Variations on a theme from Cowper

Zechariah 13:1; 2 Corinthians 8:9

'There is a fountain filled with blood
Drawn from Immanuel's veins;'
Not drawn in antiseptic vials
But spurting from nail-smashed feet and wrists,
Dripping from a barb-crowned head,
Gushing from a spear-ripped side.

This is the fountain filled with blood
Spewing from God's own veins
And sinners plunged beneath this flood
Lose all their guilty stains.

'The dying thief rejoiced to see
That fountain in his day;
And so may we, though vile as he,
Wash all our sins away.'

Wash all my sins away you say?
Wash all my sins away?
But I am good and rich and free
And sin's long passed away.

Blind fool! I say, for your state's worse
Than any thief I say;
For you are poor and proud and bound
And sin looks here to stay.

This God though rich left heaven's throne
A cowshed to adorn;
That we though poor may riches gain
And find whole worlds our own.

May you my friend such riches find,
Bloodied though they be;
For not till plunged beneath that flood
Will you be good and free.

With thanks to William Cowper, *There is a fountain filled with blood*

# The Garden

'A young man, wearing nothing but a linen garment, was following Jesus. When they seized him, he fled naked, leaving his garment behind.' (Mark 14:51–52) (NIV)

What dreadful shame
that he needs flee
naked from the garden.
If only he had stood with God
resisting all temptation.

But naked we
can now be clothed
for He stood firm, unshaken;
an entry guaranteed by God
to that celestial garden.

# The Chief Priests Chose For Power

Mark 15

The chief priests chose for power,
Pilate chose to please;
The crowd chose for a killer,
He chose to die for peace.

The soldiers chose to mock him,
How right their kingly hails;
The robbers chose to taunt him,
He chose the way of nails.

But Joseph loved him boldly,
The women followed too;
Choose now to love or leave him:
His love abounds for you.

# Barrack Room: Matthew 27:24–31

Oh my bruised and battered Lord
Naked 'cept for prop and crown
What have you done to earn these cheers?
These blows to head, this dressing down?

They couldn't care who's right, who's wrong
They couldn't care the reason
Safely sealed behind closed doors
They'll play their man for a season.

This barrack room testosterone
Smelling sweat and fear
Makes them men for a moment
Boasting lust-filled jeer.

They glory in their pleasures
They bow before His throne:
But now the curtain's opened
Their shame's exposed to all
The word's got out – unbinding –
Their sin is shamed the more:
Until it's washed and whitened
By the very blood it draws.

Good Friday, 2008

## Stormstiller

Sent to preach he sleeps run out,
Raising a storm
Only stilled by his throwing over –
So that sailors more terrified
Are hushed to worship.

Another loves us Ninevites
And sleeps swamped,
Yet stills a storm with a word –
So that sailors more terrified
Are hushed to worship.

For mercy the first is rescued
So we the rescuer see:
By his throwing over
And spewing forth
We reign on his throne storm-free.

With thanks to Tim Keller

# The New Jonah

Acts 27

Though storm conspire to stop this word
reaching the empire: Jew and Greek
Though ship go down the word goes on –
this faithful Jonah saves his ship.

The torrents rage, the waters roar
Fourteen days no star no sun
Cargo, tackle overboard
The lifeboat's cut, the anchors gone.

His passion for their souls he stands
He rescues those who plan to kill
Chained he prays unchained they'll be
and breaks the bread to show his trust
So strengthened all make safe the shore
As was his promise: Fear no more.

With thanks to Chris Green, *The Word of His Grace*

# For Sandy and Sal

A little one is on its way –
we hope!
if it can only hang in there
and grow and grow.

Lord, keep it safe:
it'll have a home that's full of care;
make it strong
and whole and yours,
a kingdom child and heir.

## Skyspinners

Genesis 1

Galileo disabused us of our notion
That the sun and all the heavenly spheres spin
'Round us –
So minimising men
And making them fear the forces that surround.

But a more careful reading tells
That sun, moon and stars were made to spin
For Him. No! For us!
So we might live – for Him
To whom all lights owe light.

# Embracing Peniel

Genesis 32:22–32

Little boys laugh and giggle
as they wrestle with their father on the lawn:
his massive hands restrained in love,
carefully making his measure –
yet their whole joy grows.

Teenagers tease and pick on their friends
and wrestle to prove their strength, their love:
at the slightest hint of hurt
they pull back
and clumsily, tenderly care.

Throughout the night, alone,
a sullied man wrestles
and cannot win, nor is he won;
to find his hip hurts, at a touch,
and to know, 'My God!' it's been my God
whose so restraint
safely embraces –
almost in a kiss –
and grows and grows.

With thanks to Graham Baird, Matthew Anstey and Gerard Manley Hopkins, *Carrion Comfort*

# A Father's Love

Do you remember when we'd collect bush-rock out near Kenthurst
and pick wildflowers you showed me how to press
under those old encyclopaedias
and mount with razor cuts in spiral-bound sketchbooks?

Do you remember laying out the polar landscape with chicken wire:
plastered, painted, modelled with icebergs and igloos
and fur-skinned Eskimos with harpoons
in balsa kayaks?

Do you remember mooing for the cow
and teaching me to run my fingers down her teats,
play-squirting the warm milk into my open mouth
and straining the full buckets,
collecting clotted cream for home-made porridge?

Do you remember flying kites that always caught,
making model aeroplanes and painting them
from little tins, soaking off their transfers?

Do you remember wrestling on the lawn:
the giant crab with flailing limbs
we'd danger dare approach till 'Caught!',
squeezed squealing with giggling delight?

Do you remember bringing home stamps from far-flung isles,
perfect mint sets tenderly chosen at airport post offices
on busy stopovers with awkward change;
delicately mounted in careful order:
tweezer-twinned with their used cousins?

I remember.
More and more.
And am thankful.
More and more.

Do you remember Bony
and *The Man From Snowy River*,
*In Crocodile Land*
and the stuffed beast we loved
with marble eyes and vicious teeth –
shot in the snout
floating in top-end muddied mangroves?

Do you remember standing on windswept fields
watching endless football games
waiting
for the boy who never scored
who couldn't catch or kick or throw?

Do you remember making cheese on toast or baked beans
after yet another baby
and do you remember cleaning up after a sick boy cries
'Da-ad'
in the dead of night
dressing-gowned, your naked body clumsily exposed?

Do you remember sandy summers at Paradise
teaching me to surf,
throwing me before the waves;
to fish,
my wicker basket full of tangled lines
with little sinkers wrapped round cork;
to row,
in varnished dinghies stowed in boathouses
smelling of salty canvas, musty sails?

Do you remember beautiful, leathered daggers, greasebladed,
    skewered;
the red headdress,
the cards from the king of Jordan,
the weddings with almonds,
the flagpole – never raised,
the Corps de Consul plates – gloveboxed
for fear,
the telephone clicks, the calls from ASIO,
the cops who visited twice a day:
the cost
of standing up for those whose voice was never heard?

I remember.
More and more.
And am thankful.
More and more.

Do you remember panning at Sapphire:
shaking the sieves,
pulling the caravan behind the old black Holden
stuck on Mt Victoria,
our bluestone booty stored for years
'midst fridgetop clutter –
whatever happened to that jar?

Do you remember training to Adelaide
and picking up the yellow Kombi
which wasn't meant to be yellow,
and flying the milk run to Cloncurry,
landing in locusts, sleeping in stars?

Do you remember exploring the Atherton
finding old airstrips their secrets forgotten
and do you remember the cage at the mine –
the samples of moly, flaking steel shine?

Do you remember teaching me to travel on our first trip
together –
selling sapphires in hotel rooms,
pulled up rapids by agile Filipinos,
breakfasting at massive Bahraini tables,
climbing the Acropolis with icy pools in Parthenon stones,
dining from freezers filled with Scottish game?

Do you remember driving in to the office on Martin Place
when people still worked on Saturday mornings
before it moved to Clarence St with that big back safe filled
   with pink-ribboned files
and then to 163 where I'd join you for drinks after work
around the panelled boardroom table?

Do you remember preaching at Castle Hill Meths
with those faithful old-timers fundraising from their cake stalls,
dressing us all up and carting us off to Sunday School
in that house trucked in next to the church
where we'd singalong
like the Sallies at Thornleigh
calling out our favourites
from *The Methodist Hymnal*
telling out the old, old story
of how the Saviour died for me?

Oh the wonder of grace,
the kindness of God,
For the preacher, the prayer, the singer, the poet,
For the rower, the player, the feaster, the man,
For the lawyer, the builder, the miner, the farmer,
For the host of the party, the friend and the father,
Who couldn't help but give,
Who couldn't help but love.

I remember.
More and more.
And am thankful.
more and more.

# Making the New Man

Generations of Presbyterians look down in black and white.
They gave their lives in sacrifice:
Sensible and sharp.
And every step away is a betrayal,
Bounded by the whip of well-learned scripts.
And every step back is plagiarism, a breach of copyright.

Thank God for Mum's gentle grace
And ready, steady care.
Thank God for her iconoclasm:
No pretensions here.
It's read as reaction, but this jester is no fool,
For her quick wit fast finds fake fronts
And my guess is its prophecy.

But truth telling doesn't build a life –
A new life, in a new home;
A new birth: just as messy and painful and vulnerable,
Only now with a greater wealth of ingredients.

Wrestling with Mum and Dad.
Wrestling between Mum and Dad.
And which one's God?
Exploring, pushing, afraid of the limits.
What fearful chasm lies beyond?
What no-man's land? What desert?

Whoa! Whoa! Whoa!
Who's cracking the whip here?
Such a fine spirit needs gentler handling,
Such a fine soul deserves greater care.

For gold isn't smithed in a day
And this gold is but dust compared to our promise.
A better alchemist is working:
Crafting a whole new jewel from the old amalgam
Breathing a whole new life:
Yet unknown, yet undreamed.
For truth telling does build lives
In paradox and play.

And are they really all that tough?
Perhaps they're not so divine as your imaginings
But in their care long too for you
To find your joy in Him;
To bravely pipe the newest path
In the new world yet unknown
And find the freedom, the space, the place
To be your wonderful self
In brilliant subtle colours.

# The Motherless Man

Genesis 24:62–66

A motherless man
Grieving in an evening field
Looks up
To see her riding in a caravan
And discovers
He has been given
The beautiful one:
Generous and bold,
A virgin
Whom he loves –
Mother of many nations.

# On the Ordination of a Friend

Galatians 3:13–14

'Oh who am I,
That for my sake
My Lord should take
Frail flesh, and die?'

Oh who am I,
for my frail flesh
is spoiled
and wrestles
with the tree,
that I should have hands laid on me
to bring His news
of life and joy
and lead His people
to that tree?

Oh who am I,
that my Great God
should use frail flesh
to win His way, His work,
through me?

Lay hands on me,
my Lord, my God
and so direct my thoughts and words.
Lay hands on me
and give me strength
to know that you are God;
that you will give
and build and grow
and bless with joy through me.

Lay hands on me,
my Christ, my God
and heal my hidden wounds,
my shadows
and my darker self,
frail flesh by death made new.

Lay hands on me,
my Friend, my Love
and hold me tight
and love me always, yes, despite;
and comfort me when I am down
and hurt
and long to sob, and hide.

Lay hands on me,
whose hand has writ
such seamless beauty in His worlds
and catch me up in your great work
of writing all things new.

Lay hands on me,
my Hope, my Shield
and give me grace to wipe away
the sticky webs of men
who cannot read your work;
that free and clean
I'll be your man,
weaving a new cloth,
wearing a new suit,
piping a new tune:
Come follow with me.

With thanks to Samuel Crossman, *My Song is Love Unknown*

# Towpath Symphony

Princeton, New Jersey

In failing light
Geese honk discordantly –
New music so beautifully attuned;
Deer stumble and crash alert
Black squirrels scuffle in rustling leaves
A duck quacks
Geese honk discordantly.

The dinky hoots
The traffic hums
The eights swish and flick, swish and flick
Interrupted by a megaphone;
The joggers pass
Thudding and huffing in time
And the rhythmic pace of man treads on, treads on.

But what man could such a symphony make?
O come, let us adore Him,
O come, let us adore Him,
O come, let us adore Him,
Christ the Lord.

# Brokenback

Pokolbin, New South Wales

The giant dinosaur sleeps
still, unperturbed
nestling the leafy green bowl of rowed vines
within its limbs;
its camouflage coat of grey brown spotted gum
crested by a spiky backbone
contouring the sky.

Oblivious to the rising drones of cicadas,
totally impervious to the hot heat building baking
charging to strobes of lightning
and cracks of thunder
stormwashing its sides;
just occasionally cleaning, tidying
licking its folded skin with warm breath
flaming flaring smoke snorting.

It slumbers still. Rock-strong and solid.
Unmoved
for aeons.
Resting –
to rise and greet Him
when we meet Him
in the air.

Romans 8:19; 1 Thessalonians 4:17

# Acknowledgements

These poems had their genesis during a study leave generously supported by Ridley College and the Australian Research Theology Foundation. Thanks must also go to family and friends who have listened patiently and encouraged me in this creative endeavour. The faculty at Gordon-Conwell and Princeton Seminaries, especially those in Preaching and Pastoral Care have taught me more than I could ever name, and my original teachers in Hopkins, Donne and David Campbell – Kath White, Jeff Ware and Rod West – opened worlds continually expanding in their richness, comfort and delight.

'Memories of Beograd' was first published in *Eureka Street* Vol. 16 No. 6 13 June 2006; 'Loneliness' was first published in *Family Ministry* Vol. 16 No. 4 Winter 2002; 'High Wire' was first published in *The Journal of Pastoral Care and Counseling* Vol. 57 No. 4 Winter 2003; 'Anna' was first published in *The Journal of Pastoral Care and Counseling* Vol. 57 No. 2 Summer 2003 under the title 'For Tim and Poppy' and subsequently in *Special Visions: Poems by and for Pastoral Caregivers* (ed. Orlo C. Strunck, Lincoln, NE: iUniverse, 2007); and 'Embracing Peniel' was first published in *Crucible: Theology and Ministry* (www.crucible.org.au) Vol. 1 No. 1 May 2008.

www.ingramcontent.com/pod-product-compliance
Lightning Source LLC
Chambersburg PA
CBHW062153100526
44589CB00014B/1818